MISSOURI

WITHDRAWN

Doug Sanders

Cavendish
Square

New York

Published in 2014 by Cavendish Square Publishing, LLC
303 Park Avenue South, Suite 1247, New York, NY 10010

Website: cavendishsq.com

This publication represents the opinions and views of the authors based on their personal experience, knowledge, and research. The information in this book serves as a general guide only. The authors and publisher have used their best efforts in preparing this book and disclaim liability rising directly or indirectly from the use and application of this book.

CPSIA Compliance Information: Batch #WW14CSQ

All websites were available and accurate when this book was sent to press.

Library of Congress Cataloging-in-Publication Data

Sanders, Doug, 1972-
  Missouri / Doug Sanders.
    pages cm. — (It's my state)
  Includes index.
  ISBN 978-1-62712-240-5 (hardcover) ISBN 978-1-62712-495-9 (paperback) ISBN 978-1-62712-251-1 (ebook)
  1. Missouri—Juvenile literature. I. Title.

  F466.3.S255 2014
  977.8—dc23

                    2013033719

This edition developed for Cavendish Square Publishing by RJF Publishing LLC (www.RJFpublishing.com)
Series Designer, Second Edition: Tammy West/Westgraphix LLC
Editorial Director: Dean Miller
Editor: Sara Howell
Copy Editor: Cynthia Roby
Art Director: Jeffrey Talbot
Layout Design: Erica Clendening
Production Manager: Jennifer Ryder-Talbot

Text, maps, and illustrations copyright © 2014 by Cavendish Square Publishing, LLC.
Maps and illustrations by Chistopher Santoro.

The photographs in this book are used by permission and through the courtesy of: Cover (main), pp. 4 (bottom), 19 (top), 44 Shutterstock.com; cover (inset) © Shutterstock; p. 4 (top) Gary W. Carter; p. 5 (top) Photo Researchers, Inc.: Mark A. Schneider; p. 5 (bottom) Susumu Sato; pp. 8, 14, 16, 47, 52, 53, 57, 62, 74 Missouri Division of Tourism; pp. 9, 13, 15 Wikimedia Commons; p. 10 Macduff Everton/Getty Images; pp. 11, 22, 32, 33, 38, 50 (top) Corbis; p. 17 Tom Brakefield/Getty Images; p. 18 (top) Animals Animals: Fred Whitehead; p. 18 (bottom) Suzanne L. & Joseph T. Collins; p. 19 (bottom) Richard Parker; p. 20 Alan & Sandy Carey; p. 21 John Conrad; pp. 25, 28 Art Resource, NY: Smithsonian American Art Museum, Washington DC; p. 29 Historical Picture Archive; p. 31 FPG/Getty Images; pp. 35, 37, 50 (bottom) Bettmann; p. 40 Historic Map Works LLC/Getty Images; p. 42 Robertstock/Retrofile: Wisconsin Historical Society; p. 46 Blend Images/John Fedele/Getty Images; p. 48 Rick Gayle; p. 49 Hulton Archive/Getty Images; p. 51 (top) Helga Esteb/Shutterstock.com; p. 54 Ted Spiegel; p. 55 John Fedele/Getty Images; p. 56 Terrance Klassen/Getty Images; p. 58 Superstock: Richard Cummins; p. 60 Aneal Vohra; p. 64 Richard Cummins; pp. 68, 69, 72 (bottom) Picture Quest: Ed Lallo/Index Stock Imagery; p. 70 Buddy Mays; p. 71 Color Image, Inc.; p. 72 (top) Ed Lallo/ZUMA; p. 72 (middle) Kent Dufault; p. 73 (top) Lester V. Bergman; p. 73 (bottom) Omni Photo Communications Inc.

Every effort has been made to locate the copyright holders of the images used in this book.

Printed in the United States of America.

MISSOURI

CONTENTS

THE SHOW-ME STATE

State Tree: Flowering Dogwood

This elegant tree can grow more than 30 feet (9.1 m) tall. It was adopted as the state tree in 1955. The tree grows in clusters across the state, but is most often found in the Ozarks and in several counties north of the Missouri River.

State Bird: Bluebird

As its name suggests, this delicate songbird is known for its striking blue feathers. A bluebird usually reaches about 6 to 7 inches (15–17.8 cm) in length. Throughout the twentieth century, the nation's bluebird population started to quickly shrink. Concerned Missourians stepped in, putting up thousands of nesting boxes to help the species along. So far their efforts have met with success.

State Mineral: Galena

Galena is a major source of lead ore. It was adopted as the state's mineral in 1967 to acknowledge Missouri as the top lead producer in the United States. Galena also contains silver and is an important ore in silver mining.

State Fossil: Crinoid

Fossilized crinoids are the remains of animals that lived millions of years ago. Because a crinoid sometimes looks similar to a plant, it has earned the nickname sea lily. Related to the starfish and the sand dollar, crinoids lived in the vast sea that once covered the state. Today there are about 600 species of crinoid living in the world's oceans.

State Reptile: Three-Toed Box Turtle

In 2007, the three-toed box turtle was declared the state reptile. These animals are native to the south-central United States and are often kept as pets. They get their name from the three toes on their back feet.

State Musical Instrument: Fiddle

Fur traders first brought the fiddle to Missouri in the late 1700s. Playing music was a main source of entertainment, and a fiddle player was highly respected for his or her talents. The instrument, which helped shape the state's rich musical heritage, was officially adopted in 1987.

MISSOURI

Missouri River

St. Joseph

Revere

Hannibal

Mississippi River

Columbia

Mark Twain Lake

St. Charles

Independence

Kansas City

Jefferson City

Missouri River

St. Louis

Lake of the Ozarks

Harry S. Truman Reservoir

Bridal Cave

Gasconade River

Meramec River

TAUM SAUK MOUNTAIN

Osage River

Pomme de Terre Lake

ST. FRANCOIS MOUNTAINS

JOHNSON'S SHUT-INS STATE PARK

Cape Girardeau

Spring River

Stockton Lake

Springfield

Joplin

MARK TWAIN NATIONAL FOREST

POPLAR BLUFF

Lake Wappapello

Mississippi River

Table Rock Lake

Branson

N

W   E

S

The Show-Me State

Missouri is a state at the crossroads. It is where the western prairie meets the eastern woodlands and where the northern plains join the lowlands of the Southeast. It is also where two of the nation's mightiest rivers, the Missouri and the Mississippi, join forces. Countless settlers once rolled across this land, earning the city of St. Louis (or Saint Louis) the nickname "Gateway to the West." Many people passed through this gateway and continued west, while others stayed to build lives in the heartland. Missourians only have to look around them to see the gifts their state has to offer. Rushing streams, lush forests, and glistening lakes are just some of the reasons millions of visitors arrive each year, declaring, "Show me Missouri."

The Northern Plains

Although the great Mississippi River unrolls along Missouri's eastern border, as far as geography is concerned, the state's most important waterway is the Missouri River. The source of the river is

Quick Facts

Missouri's Borders

North	Iowa
South	Arkansas
East	Illinois
	Kentucky
	Tennessee
West	Kansas
	Nebraska
	Oklahoma

far to the west of the state, in Montana. There it flows strong and clear. By the time the river reaches Missouri its color has usually changed. Murky and dark, the river picks up dirt and silt as it winds its way to the Mississippi. For this reason, the Missouri has earned the nickname, the Big Muddy.

The Big Muddy acts as a natural dividing point. It creates a rough border between northern and southern Missouri and splits the state in two, with the bottom being the somewhat larger part. The Big Muddy also helps to divide the state's landscape. Though dense forests, low hills, and vast grasslands are found across the state, each section of Missouri has its own unique sense of beauty.

The Missouri River drains one-sixth of the United States. It flows 2,341 miles (3,767 km) from its source in Montana to where it joins the Mississippi River near St. Louis.

This flowstone formation, called Blondie's Throne, is part of Marvel Cave, near Branson.

The Northern Plains are also called the central lowlands. These lowlands include the parts of Missouri north of the Missouri River, as well as parts of Iowa, Nebraska, and Kansas. Hundreds of thousands of years ago, the Northern Plains of Missouri were covered by glaciers. As the massive chunks of ice eventually headed north, they left behind soil rich in nutrients and mineral deposits. Today northern Missouri is ideal farm country. Corn and soybeans thrive among the rolling grasslands, and cattle graze the fields.

Because of all this Ice-Age action, this part of the state is also called the dissected till plains. That is because the glaciers tilled, or ground and mashed up, tiny pieces of rock and soil. Once the glaciers had left the region, rivers and streams dissected, or cut through, the smooth surface of the till plains. Today the Northern Plains are a series of river valleys bordered by higher, hill country.

In some sections, though, the land levels off to become almost perfectly flat. These areas bear traces of the original till plain. The flattest part of the Northern Plains is found in a narrow strip just west of the Mississippi River. There, the surface of the land was not broken up by water and erosion.

All in all, the Northern Plains are a blend of forest and prairie. A variety of trees, mostly oaks, huddle near the sparkling rivers and cover the backs of the gentle hills. Farther away from the river valleys, prairie grasses stretch for great distances, set off by small clusters of trees.

The western part of the state's central lowlands is formed by the Osage Plains. These plains also stretch into Kansas, Oklahoma, and Texas. Missouri's portion of the Osage Plains features some low hills and wide, shallow valleys that interrupt its flat, even appearance. Because the Osage Plains were glacier free, the soil there is not as rich. The area is still a productive farming region, though. Coal mining is another important industry in the region.

Aside from being an important transportation waterway, the Missouri River also provides many fun activities, such as kayaking and canoeing.

To many residents and visitors alike, the Missouri landscape offers the ideal blend—gentle rivers, rolling hills, and towering clusters of hardwood trees.

The Ozark Plateau

The Ozark Plateau makes up the largest part of the state. It covers most of southern Missouri and reaches into Arkansas and Oklahoma. Filled with steep-sloped ridges, deep ravines, and clear, fast-flowing streams, the Ozark Plateau has it all. Low mountains and rugged forest-covered hills add to the region's variety and make it one of the Midwest's most popular vacation spots.

The Ozark Plateau is shaped like a huge dome, or an upside-down bowl. Gently rising, it slowly gains altitude. The highest section is found in the southwest where the land reaches heights of around 1,700 feet (518 m). This part of the plateau extends northeast, ending in the St. Francois Mountains. To the southeast, the Ozark Plateau descends sharply. By the time the plateau reaches the plains bordering the Mississippi River, the land is about 400 feet (122 m) above sea level.

The St. Francois Mountains stretch above the horizon. They are ancient volcanoes that erupted millions of years ago. When this part of the Midwest was covered by water, these mountains probably looked like towering islands rising out of an ancient sea. Today most of the rock found in the rest of the region has been worn away by water and wind. In its place are the rounded domes, spiky knobs, and granite peaks that together cover about 70 square miles (181 sq km).

The St. Francois Mountains do not form one continuous chain. Instead they rise in small groups of usually two to three mountains. Then the land levels off only to Taum Sauk Mountain, the state's highest point reaching 1,772 feet (540 m) above sea level.

At one time, millions of years ago, the land stretching across southern Missouri was unbroken. Since then, however, streams have been slicing valleys into the Ozark Plateau. They have also shaped much more than the state's surface. Most of the Ozark Plateau is made up of limestone and dolomite. These are two types of rocks formed by layers of tiny particles that are pressed and crushed together. With so many underground rivers in this part of the state, water has slowly eaten away at the layers. Over the years it has sculpted the rock to create a fascinating maze beneath the Show-Me State. Together thousands of caves, springs, and sinkholes form Missouri's underground world of wonders.

This plaque sits atop Taum Sauk Mountain, declaring it the highest point in Missouri.

Quick Facts

The area around Big Spring was one of Missouri's first state parks. In 1969, the land was donated by the state to the National Parks Service to become part of the Ozark National Scenic Riverways.

The state is well known for its caves. More than 1,450 of them fan out into long tunnels and magnificent, sprawling caverns. With 10 miles (16 km) of passageways, Marvel Cave, near Branson, is one of the largest. Meramec Caverns in Stanton is another top spot for cave lovers.

Just as impressive are the state's natural springs. About 10,000 of them gurgle and bubble out of the plateau. They are of varying sizes, but more than 100 springs each give off more than 1 million gallons (3.8 million L) of water per day. Big Spring, near Van Buren, tops all of them, releasing about 286 million gallons (1.08 billion L) of water each day.

Taking their place in this watery world are the many reservoirs and lakes that dot the Ozark Plateau. The state's second-largest body of water, Lake of the Ozarks, is the crown jewel of southern Missouri. It covers about 55,300 acres (22,379 ha). Many Missourians love to cruise its waters in their boats. In summer, residents and visitors spend lazy afternoons chugging along meeting and greeting the other outdoor lovers drawn to this sprawling manmade lake.

Created as part of the Great Osage River Project, Lake of the Ozarks appeared on the map in the early 1930s after Bagnell Dam was completed. The dam project employed more than 20,000 people during the two years it took to complete.

The Harry S. Truman Dam, on the Osage River, creates the state's largest lake, called Truman Reservoir.

The Bootheel

For such a tiny portion of the state, this region has certainly earned a lot of names. Also called the southeastern lowlands or the gulf coastal plains, the Mississippi Alluvial Plains mark the flat area beside the river where floodwaters reach. The word alluvial refers to all the sand, silt, minerals, and nutrients the floodwaters leave behind each year. Because of all these rich deposits, this is the most fertile part of the state. It is also the flattest, with a few low ridges breaking up the landscape here and there.

Despite its many names, when most Missourians refer to the region, they simply call it the Bootheel. It gets its name from its shape, which resembles the thick heel of a cowboy boot. Before settlers arrived, the Bootheel was covered in water that surrounded the dense, swampy forests. Through the years, settlers cleared and drained the area and turned it into a prime farming region. Today cotton, soybeans, corn, and rice thrive in the area.

Climate

As native Missourians often say, "If you don't like the weather, wait an hour, and it'll change." Missouri has a variable climate, meaning it is subject to a range of temperatures. In the hilly or mountainous areas, winters and summers tend to be milder than in regions with lower elevations. Residents in the southeast can expect about 50 inches (127 cm) of precipitation per year. Precipitation is all the moisture that falls, usually in the form of rain and snow. Missourians who live in the northwest receive far less precipitation with about 30 inches (76 cm) per year.

Summers in the state tend to be long, warm, and humid with the sticky weather sometimes lasting from June to September. The highest temperature recorded in the state is 118°F (47.8°C). This mark was hit three different times, on July 15 and 18, 1936, and on July 14, 1954.

Winters are both brief and unpredictable. They are rarely severe and may even feature brief periods of warmth. In the middle of winter, it is not uncommon

Many Missourians enjoy the winter. Snow makes an occasional appearance, but heavy blizzards and long periods of severe cold are rare.

to have pleasant days when the temperature reaches between 50°F and 60°F (10–15.5°C). These patches of warmth can just as easily be followed by periods of severe cold. The state's record low temperature is -40°F (-40°C), recorded in Warsaw on February 13, 1905.

Wild Missouri

Forests cover about one-third of Missouri. They are generally found in the southern part of the state and in the river valleys of the north. Mostly hardwoods, a majority of the Show-Me State's trees come from the oak and hickory families. Sweet gum, bald cypress, cottonwoods, elms, and maples are present in large numbers, too.

In springtime, the Ozark Plateau is a wildflower paradise. Flowers native to the state include violets, anemones, buttercups, wild roses, phlox, asters, columbines, and goldenrods, to name just a few. A short walk through any of Missouri's wild stretches will reveal many more.

Woodchucks thrive in the flower-filled fields of Missouri. Avid plant eaters, a spring meadow offers these small mammals an unlimited feast.

Armadillo

Missouri has a small but growing population of these animals. About the size of a housecat and with a tough, protective shell, an armadillo is a good swimmer and can walk underwater for up to six minutes. When startled, it can leap into the air.

Channel Catfish

The channel catfish is the official state fish. Slender with a forked tail, the species does not rely on its sight to find food. Instead it uses its catlike whiskers to feel out a possible meal. Adults can grow up to 32 inches (81 cm) long and weigh up to 15 pounds (6.8 kg).

Ozark Zigzag Salamander

The Ozark zigzag tends to live on the damp floor of Missouri's forests. It burrows among moist leaves or under rotting logs. This brownish amphibian can reach up to 4 inches (10.2 cm) in length and is known for the thin purple stripe down its back. The species is now protected in most states.

Grape

Missouri's warm summers and rocky soil are perfect for grape-growing. Though they can be eaten off the vine, grapes are often grown and used to make wine. Missouri's wine industry was started by Germans who immigrated to the territory in the early 1800s. In the early part of the twentieth century, Missouri was one of the biggest wine producers in the country and there are more than 100 wineries in the state today. Missouri has even declared a grape as one of its official state symbols!

Missouri Gooseberry

This shrub grows mostly in moist, wooded ravines. Its greenish white flowers appear in March or April, followed by a crop of berries, which dot the bush from June to September. The berries are a favorite food among birds, but people enjoy them as well. Some Missouri cooks turn the juicy gooseberries into delicious jams and jellies.

Pawpaw

The pawpaw is found across the state, except in the northernmost parts. It can reach 30 feet (9.1 m) in height and thrives in the moist soils along streams. The fruit ripens in the early autumn. It is eaten by birds, raccoons, opossums, squirrels, and the occasional human.

With so much variety in its terrain, it is not surprising that the state is home to a wide range of animals. In the state's forests and along its grassy plains, cottontail rabbits, beavers, foxes, squirrels, raccoons, and opossums all share the land's resources. White-tailed deer sneak out of the cover of trees to munch grass in the fields.

Birds are drawn to Missouri's mild climate and the food the wilderness provides. Mockingbirds, purple finches, woodpeckers, and blue jays fill the air with their songs. They nest in the trees and shrubs that grow across the state.

With 56,000 miles (90,123 km) of streams within its borders, Missouri's waterways are filled with fish. Bass, bluegills, catfish, crappies, and trout add to the aquatic variety, much to the joy of many state residents. Missouri is fishing country. Bass Pro Shop, a fishing and outdoor recreation retailer, has its headquarters in Springfield.

Raccoons can be found in the state's forests. They also occassionally appear in Missouri's cities and towns, too.

White-tailed deer have adapted well to the variety of habitats the state offers. With plenty of food to choose from, this fawn will soon be towering over the daisies.

Though Missourians take great care of their state, many of its animals have been threatened through the years. With the spread of suburbs and more and more land being developed, some animals were losing their homes. State scientists and officials became concerned when population levels for these animals started to decline. So they came up with a plan to reverse this trend, and so far their efforts have paid off. State conservation workers have been successful in building up Missouri's population of once-threatened species such as white-tailed deer, wild turkeys, and otters. These are just three of the success stories, but they serve as proof of Missourians' love for their state and their desire to be sure all of its residents—both human and nonhuman—thrive.

From the Beginning

Nomadic hunters first wandered Missouri in search of game about 12,000 years ago. Called Paleo-Indians, these people were the ancestors of the Native Americans who would eventually spread across North America. The Paleo-Indians camped in simple, short-term shelters while hunting or searching for food. For many years, very little was known about the Paleo-Indians. Scientists have only recently been able to piece together a more complete picture of Paleo-Indian life. One important discovery was the Kimmswick Bone Bed at Mastodon State Historic Site, in Imperial. The site has offered some valuable artifacts. Clovis points, which are a kind of spear tip, and other stone tools were found along with the remains of a mastodon, a huge prehistoric creature that was often hunted. The site offered the first proof that mastodons had lived during the time of the Paleo-Indians. Valuable finds such as these provide an important glimpse into a mysterious and far-distant past.

Gradually the Paleo-Indians formed more complex communities. By 3000 BC, Missouri's early residents were making baskets and had developed a variety of stone tools. Pottery was introduced to the region, followed by an even more important addition—agriculture. Farming meant that people could settle into more permanent villages and establish more stable lives.

The child of a sharecropper reads in her family's cabin in New Madrid County in this photograph from 1938. During hard years or times of prosperity, Missourians have always been able to make a living out of the land.

The Native Past

After the Paleo-Indians, another group of people, called the Mound Builders, settled in the region. In present-day Missouri, these people rose to power along the Mississippi River valley. Today, there are traces of their once–bustling urban center, Cahokia, just across the Mississippi River in west-central Illinois. Experts estimate that the city had a population of about 20,000 around the year AD 1100. In the center of the city stood a huge flat-topped mound standing almost 100 feet tall (30.5 m). Experts believe it and the other mounds were used for burial and religious purposes and to mark important locations. The mounds might have also been used for other purposes. As many as 100 have been found in the area.

The culture of the Mound Builders gave rise to the various Native American groups that were well established in the region by the time the first European explorers arrived. Missouri's forests and prairies were filled with game, and the state offered an ideal place for these native communities to thrive. The early Native Americans spent roughly half of the year following herds of animals. The other half of the year, they settled in simple villages where they grew a variety of vegetables. The largest and most powerful group in the region was the Osage. Today the Osage River bears their name and marks the spot where this strong nation settled.

The Osage settled in the south and west of Missouri in villages made up of cone-shaped huts. Larger buildings, for meetings and ceremonies, were made of poles woven together with long strands of grass. The Osage were hunters and farmers and took advantage of all Missouri had to offer. Deer, bison, and bear were just some of the animals they hunted in the wilds of Missouri. Back in the villages, their gardens were filled with pumpkins, corn, beans, and squash.

Other groups shared the region as well. The Otoe lived north of the Missouri River. The Missouri Indians, after whom the state is named, settled mostly in the eastern and central portions of the state. Around 1790 a group of Shawnee migrated west of the Mississippi River and settled near Cape Girardeau. By 1815 more than 1,200 Shawnee lived there. They were soon joined by a large band of

This 1834 painting shows three Osage men, called He Who Takes Away, War, and Mink-chesk. The interference of the Spanish, French, and governments proved too much for this once-mighty nation, and eventually the Osage were forced out of the state.

MAKING AN OZARK NAIL RASP

The Ozark region is known for its rich traditions in music and dance. Skilled Missouri craftspeople used the strong wood from the trees along the mountains to make musical instruments such as fiddles, banjos, mountain dulcimers, and drums. On special occasions, everyone came together to sing traditional folk songs, play music, and dance a lively jig. With the help of an adult, you can make your own Ozark nail rasp, a simple musical instrument.

WHAT YOU NEED

A piece of wood, about 10 inches (25.4 cm) long, 2 inches (5 cm) wide, and 2 inches (5 cm) high

17 nails: 16 nails in 4 different sizes (4 for each size) and 1 large nail for strumming

Thick working gloves (used for yard work or gardening)

Hammer

Pencil

Ruler

Paint (optional)

Sandpaper (optional)

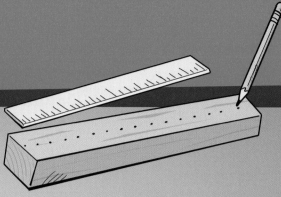

It is very important that you have an adult help you with this project. Using a hammer and nails can be dangerous. Be sure to wear your gloves while working with the wood, and be careful of splinters.

Using the ruler, draw a line with the pencil down the length of the wood. Make sixteen evenly spaced marks on the line.

Set aside the largest nail, which you will use for strumming the instrument. Separate the remaining sixteen nails into four groups according to their size. With the help of an adult, hammer the four largest nails into the first four marks, starting at either end. Watch your fingers! Do not hammer the nail in all the way—just enough to make sure it is firmly planted in the wood. Repeat with the three other groups of nails, moving from the largest to the smallest.

You can decorate your instrument by painting or sanding the wood to make an interesting shape. Once your instrument is finished, pick up the strumming nail and see what kind of music you can make on your handmade instrument.

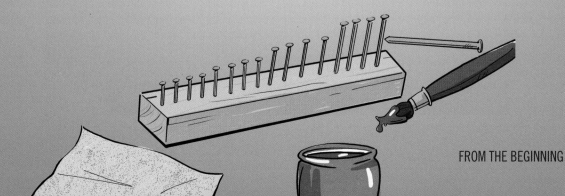

Delaware Indians, and the two groups became closely linked. Although the Osage dominated the region for years, the Iowa, and later the Sauk and Fox, became powerful in the early 1800s. They drove out rivals and controlled large stretches of territory.

Europeans Arrive

French explorers Jacques Marquette and Louis Jolliet were most likely the first Europeans to reach the mouth of the Missouri River. In 1673 they marked the spot where the Big Muddy pours into the Mississippi. They met the Peoria, a native group that offered the hungry explorers food and shelter on their long journey.

Marquette and Jolliet were soon followed by other curious explorers. In 1682 fellow Frenchman Sieur de La Salle traveled down the Mississippi River. He declared the entire valley the property of the French government. He and other

Pushed out of their homeland near the Great Lakes, the Fox and the Sauk eventually made their way to Missouri in the early 1800s.

With its two major rivers offering easy access to the region, Missouri was highly sought by trappers and settlers alike.

early explorers spoke of the natural resources Missouri and the entire midwestern region held. Some were lured with tales of gold and silver lying just beneath the surface. While French miners never found these valuable metals, they did uncover lead and salt. Their efforts were mostly focused in what is now St. Francois County where they set up a successful operation.

Trappers were also drawn to the region. They arrived and took advantage of the wealth of furbearing animals that lived in Missouri. Trade routes were set up, and soon trading posts dotted the Mississippi River valley. Large quantities of furs were sent downriver and on to the east coast and Europe. Missouri's location near two major waterways helped to speed the gradual settlement of the area.

Missionaries came as well, eager to convert the Native Americans to Catholicism. They set up several missions in the area. Around 1700, Jesuit missionaries set up Missouri's first European settlement at the Mission of St. Francis Xavier. It stood near present-day St. Louis. However, the nearby swamps posed too many threats. Disease easily spread through the mission, and the site was left behind in 1703.

The state's first permanent European settlement was founded around 1750. Settlers from Illinois crossed into Missouri and set up a small community at Sainte Genevieve. They were mostly French miners drawn to the area's rich deposits of lead. They opened the door for a string of larger and more successful communities to come. In 1764 Pierre Laclède and 13-year-old Auguste Chouteau founded St. Louis. The future city served as a trading post and as the base for their new fur empire. Avenues and districts in St. Louis still bear their names today.

Missouri was about to change hands. In a 1762 treaty, France gave all of its lands west of the Mississippi River to Spain. Missouri became a Spanish colony. The Spaniards wanted to see their new territory prosper. They encouraged settlers from the east to move in and tame the unclaimed wilderness. Hundreds came from Kentucky, Tennessee, Virginia, and the Carolinas. Among the newcomers was legendary frontiersman Daniel Boone. He arrived at St. Charles County in 1799 after the Spanish had given him 850 acres (344 ha) of land. In 1800 Boone became a syndic, or frontier judge, in the area. He grew to love his adopted state and considered himself a Missourian for the rest of his life.

Spain's control of the territory was to be short lived. In 1800 Missouri changed ownership again. France, under its leader Napoléon Bonaparte, demanded the valuable territory back. So the frontier residents once again came under French rule. By then, most of Missouri had been thoroughly explored. Communities had begun to spring up across the region. As war raged back in Europe, Napoléon and his nation found themselves in need of money. The French leader unwillingly sold the region to the United States. As part of the Louisiana Purchase, Missouri officially changed hands for its third and final time. The vast territory was divided into two parts. Missouri was included in the northern part, referred to as Upper Louisiana.

Much of Daniel Boone's extended family moved with him to Missouri. In his later years, Boone enjoyed hunting and trapping.

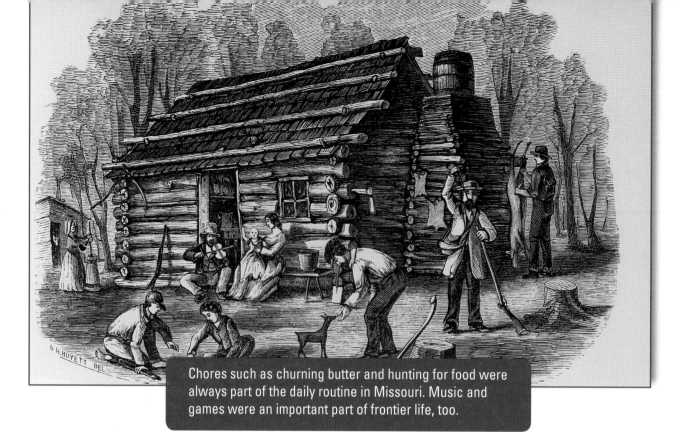

Chores such as churning butter and hunting for food were always part of the daily routine in Missouri. Music and games were an important part of frontier life, too.

The New Territory

In 1812 Congress officially made Missouri a territory. At the time, its population totaled about 20,000. Unlike other territories, Missouri already had its own bustling economy. Farmers harvested crops. Miners removed valuable ores and minerals from the rich earth. Prosperous communities continued to grow, building schools and adding churches. Word spread quickly, and many settlers were convinced that Missouri was the perfect place to live. Even more people poured into the region. The new arrivals helped the territory to grow and thrive all the more. Kansas City emerged as a new urban community as well as a center for the state's grain and livestock markets.

Pioneers also settled in Missouri's Ozark Mountains. Many came from southern states. They settled the Ozark region, building homesteads and establishing small farms and communities. Ozark residents established mills on the river and found ways to survive in the rugged terrain.

Not all the residents of the territory were happy about the growing population. With so many new arrivals, competition for land increased. Soon the area's many Native Americans were being pushed off the lands they and their ancestors had called home for hundreds of years. The state's Native Americans were slowly forced farther west. Conflicts arose. Some native groups decided to resist, launching a series of raids on the frontier settlements. Around the same time, the War of 1812 had broken out between the United States and Great Britain. In an effort to gain support and to weaken the Americans, the British gave weapons to the Native Americans. They also encouraged them to continue their attacks. The settlers responded by building more forts and making existing structures even stronger.

When the War of 1812 came to an end, the tensions did not end with it. Native Americans extended their raids into 1815 when a treaty signed at Portage des Sioux ended the fighting and took away more traditional Native American lands. It was a sign of things to come. The following year, only 5,000 Native Americans were left in the state. By 1825 the Osage had given up all of their Missouri holdings and moved to Kansas. By the late 1830s, most of the state's Native Americans had been killed, driven away, or forced onto reservations in neighboring states.

This temporary camp housed railroad workers in the Missouri countryside as they laid tracks.

The Great Compromise

In 1818 Missouri leaders asked the US Congress to make the territory a state. The request brought a unique problem to Missouri that would divide it for the next several years. In its early days, the region had been mostly settled by Southerners who had brought their slaves with them. When Missourians asked to be admitted to the Union as a slave state, though, the request triggered a growing nationwide debate.

Many people in the rest of the nation wanted Missouri to be a free state. The dispute was not decided until 1820 when Congress adopted the Missouri Compromise. Under its terms, Missouri would be admitted as a slave state if Maine entered as a free state. That way neither side, those for and against slavery, would have the greater power in Congress. So on August 10, 1821, Missouri officially became the twenty-fourth state. At the time, the new state had a population of 66,586 people, including its 10,222 slaves.

The Gateway

Missouri will long be remembered for the important role it played in the settling of the western frontier. The state was considered a starting point where many western expeditions were launched. For years the territory had been conducting a growing trade with Mexico by way of the Santa Fe Trail. This important route linked Independence, in western Missouri, with Santa Fe. Today Santa Fe is in the US state of New Mexico, but at the time it was part of Mexico. Independence became one of the leading economic centers on the frontier. Soon the Oregon Trail, which took settlers to the Pacific Northwest, also became a heavily traveled route. The Oregon Trail also started in the prosperous city of Independence. All this activity spelled greater growth for the state. By 1860 Missouri had 1.2 million residents—eighteen times the number of people the state claimed in 1820.

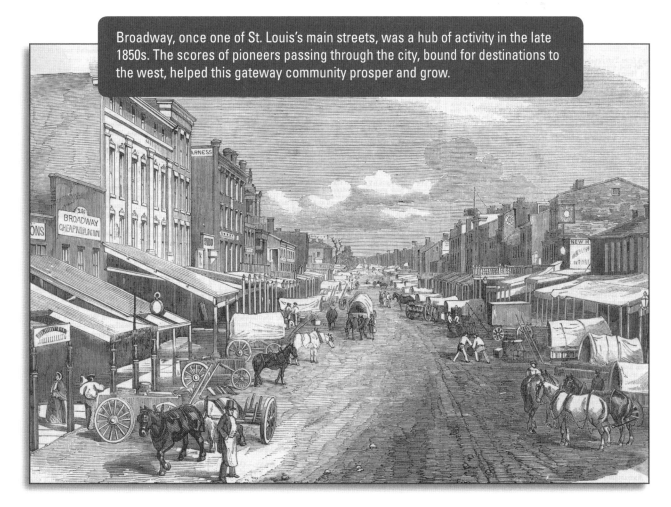

Broadway, once one of St. Louis's main streets, was a hub of activity in the late 1850s. The scores of pioneers passing through the city, bound for destinations to the west, helped this gateway community prosper and grow.

Dred Scott and the Road to War

In the 1850s a former Missouri slave took his fight for freedom all the way to the US Supreme Court. Dred Scott had moved with his owner, Dr. John Emerson, in 1836 from St. Louis to Fort Snelling, in present-day Minnesota, where slavery was not allowed. Eventually, Dr. Emerson and Dred Scott moved back to St. Louis. This action prompted Scott to argue that he was no longer a slave since he had been taken to a territory where slavery was not allowed. After pleading his case before state and federal circuit courts, the case went to the Supreme Court in Washington, D.C. In a landmark decision, the court ruled that African Americans, whether slave or free, were not US citizens and did not have the right to pursue a case in court. The decision sparked a major controversy and only increased the bitterness and tension that existed between the North and South.

These tensions hit home most noticeably in the western part of the state. Some Missourians living in the area feared that the Kansas Territory would be admitted to the Union as a free state. Many antislavery supporters had settled in Kansas, and they were determined to keep Kansas slavery free. Tensions along the Missouri–Kansas border became so high that violence soon erupted. Fighting and skirmishes would continue to grip the region until the end of the Civil War, despite the fact that Kansas was admitted to the Union in 1861 as a free state.

Though Missouri was a slave state, its officials were unsure what course the state would take when the Civil War divided the nation. Southern supporters wondered if the state would secede, or withdraw, from the Union and become a part of the Confederate States of America, the name for the group of Southern states that fought against the North. Most Missourians did not want to have to choose sides. Officials forced the issue, though. The pro-Southern governor, Claiborne F. Jackson, held a state convention to find out what plan of action Missourians wanted to adopt. After a series of meetings in February and March 1861, the members of the convention voted to stay part of the Union. Missourians wanted the fighting to stay as far away from their state as possible. This wish eventually proved impossible.

After John Emerson died, his wife married an abolitionist and Congressman named Calvin C. Chaffee. Chaffee convinced his wife to return Dred Scott, seen here, and his family to their original owners, who then set them free.

Before 1866 it was illegal to educate African Americans in the state of Missouri. The Reverend John Berry Meachum found a way around the law by taking his students out on a boat in the middle of the Mississippi and holding class.

Missourians' hopes for peace at home did not last long. When President Abraham Lincoln asked Missouri to send troops to fight for the North, Governor Jackson refused. The governor was commander of the state militia, which clashed with Union troops at Boonville on June 17, 1861. The Union troops, under the command of General Nathaniel Lyon, defeated the governor's troops and seized control of northern Missouri. Meanwhile, Jackson and his supporters regrouped in the southwestern part of the state. They then marched to Wilson's Creek near Springfield where, with the help of Confederate troops, they defeated the Union forces.

By March 7, 1862, Confederate forces controlled key positions near Pea Ridge, Arkansas. The following day, Union soldiers rallied and turned the tide of the battle. The Confederate forces retreated, and the North controlled Missouri for the next two years.

The start of the Civil War had only divided the state even more. To try and remedy this, another political convention was held. Officials decided to remove pro-Confederate leaders from office and replace them with individuals loyal to the Union cause. To begin the process, a new governor, Hamilton R. Gamble, was chosen.

Governor Jackson did not step down quietly, though. In October 1861, Jackson called a meeting of the state legislature at Neosho. Not enough legislators attended to make the meeting official, but those who did come decided to secede from the Union. As a result, the state had become geographically divided as well. Confederate forces controlled southern portions of the state, while northern parts remained loyal to the Union. In March 1862, Union troops reclaimed the southern area in a battle in nearby Pea Ridge, Arkansas. After another Confederate attempt to recapture Missouri, Southern soldiers were soundly defeated in 1864 near Kansas City. That marked the official end of fighting in Missouri. However, the rivalry and division did not go away. Small bands of pro-North and pro-South supporters would engage in combat until the end of the war. Roving groups also wandered across the countryside, burning and looting towns and killing people whom they thought disloyal to their cause.

Boom Towns

The war years marked a major change for the state in several ways. Despite the deep political divisions the state faced, Missouri thrived and continued to build its economy. Soon after the war, St. Louis and Kansas City became major business centers.

As trade along the Santa Fe Trail ended and the fur trade declined, the state's economy was forced to shift. Business leaders began looking to new sources of income. They also realized it was cheaper to process raw materials in Missouri than pay the costs to ship them to processors in the East. Soon flour and lumber mills sprang up. By the 1860s, St. Louis was producing about 500,000 barrels of flour per year. Beef, corn, oats, and apples were also processed and shipped out of the state. Factories made cloth and products of iron and lead, while breweries produced beer.

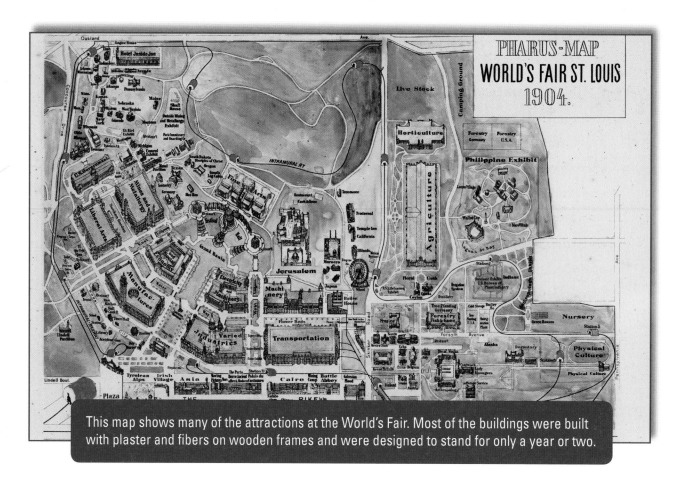

This map shows many of the attractions at the World's Fair. Most of the buildings were built with plaster and fibers on wooden frames and were designed to stand for only a year or two.

Slowly transportation routes improved. By 1870 there were about 2,000 miles (3,219 km) of railroad tracks crisscrossing the state. Soon immigrants from places such as Germany, Ireland, and Italy flocked into the state. The face of Missouri was once again changing.

Reform

The first decade of the twentieth century brought about a call for reform and statewide improvements. In 1905 Governor Joseph W. Folk took office. During his term, new laws were passed to change how elections were run and how the state did business. Another change meant Missouri's factories were to be inspected to make sure employees were given fair working conditions. Laws controlling child labor and the state's public utilities were also passed. Schools were improved, and the prison system was reformed. The state's systems of highways and roads were also expanded and improved.

In 1917, war gripped the nation once again. However, World War I actually helped boost Missouri's industries. Miners, factory workers, and farmers all increased production to make supplies for the American troops. General John J. Pershing, who was born in Linn County, was chosen to head the nation's troops in France. He was just one of thousands of Missourians fighting in the war overseas.

The arrival of the Great Depression proved a major setback for the state. During the 1930s, Missourians faced hard times. Many lost their jobs, and families struggled to make ends meet. Low crop prices spelled disaster for countless farmers. The state government cut jobs and laid off workers in an attempt to save money. Relief came in the form of federal programs. Agencies were set up to give people jobs building dams, bridges, and roads and improving public lands.

World War II and Beyond

In the 1940s, another war gave Missouri's struggling economy the jolt it needed. New industries were developed to supply the United States's armed forces fighting in Europe and Asia.

In 1944 Harry Truman, a US senator from Independence, was elected vice president. When President Franklin Roosevelt died in office in 1945, Truman stepped into the role of president. He was elected to a full term in 1948.

The 1950s saw another important shift in the state's economy. New factories and industrial plants opened across the state. Missouri enjoyed its postwar prosperity. However, new challenges were in store for both the state's cities and farms.

Starting in the early 1970s, many of Missouri's urban residents began fleeing to the suburbs, taking their tax dollars with them. This meant there was less money available for the inner cities. Crime was on the rise as well. Stretches of

Eager trainees attended "tractorette school" in Maryville in 1942, as part of a plan to teach thousands of women how to operate farm machinery. With so many men off fighting in World War II, women on the homefront stepped in to plant and harvest the much-needed crops.

St. Louis began to look like a ghost town. Buildings became neglected and were in need of repair. Once again, the cities were facing a turning point.

Those living in rural areas faced their own trials as well. During the 1980s, Missouri continued to lose its farms at an alarming rate. Farms proved too difficult—and expensive—for many families to maintain. Despite these problems, the 1990s were a time of rebuilding and economic growth. Cities formed plans to rebuild their downtown areas and to encourage new businesses. While farming declined, resourceful Missourians once again found new ways of earning an income.

Today, Missouri stands firmly committed to improving schools, protecting the environment, and building its economy. Despite the setbacks, farming and farm products are still an important part of the state's economy. New businesses and industries have moved into the state as well. Missourians know that if they remain strong and are able to change with the times, they can look to the future with confidence, proud to live in their beloved Show-Me State.

Important Dates

★ **1500s** The Delaware, Shawnee, Osage, and other native groups live in present-day Missouri.

★ **1673** Explorers Jacques Marquette and Louis Jolliet arrive in Missouri.

★ **1724** Fort Orleans is built on the north bank of the Missouri River.

★ **1750** Missouri's first permanent European settlement is founded at Sainte Genevieve.

★ **1804** Meriwether Lewis and William Clark leave St. Louis to begin exploring the lands acquired in the Louisiana Purchase.

★ **1811–1812** The most powerful series of earthquakes to strike the United States occurs in southeastern Missouri.

★ **1812** The Missouri Territory is established.

★ **1820** The Missouri Compromise settles differences over whether the territory would allow slavery.

★ **1821** Missouri is admitted to the Union as the twenty-fourth state.

★ **1825** The Osage Indians turn the last of their lands over to the United States government and move west into Kansas.

★ **1841** The first settlers leave Independence bound for the Oregon Trail.

★ **1851** The state's first railroad is built.

★ **1854** Border wars ignite between Kansans and Missourians over the issue of slavery.

★ **1857** The Supreme Court rules that Dred Scott would remain a slave, even though he had lived in free territories.

★ **1860** The Pony Express begins operation, with riders heading west from St. Joseph.

★ **1904** St. Louis hosts both the Olympics and the Louisiana Purchase Exposition, often called the World's Fair.

★ **1931** The Osage River is dammed, creating Lake of the Ozarks.

★ **1965** The Gateway Arch is completed in St. Louis.

★ **1993** A major flood threatens residents along the Mississippi River valley.

★ **2001** Missourian John Ashcroft is named United States attorney general.

★ **2011** The deadliest tornado to strike the United States in 60 years occurs in Joplin.

The People

Since its earliest days, Missouri has been a blend of cultures and ethnic traditions. Most of the state's initial settlers were American-born families of Scotch-Irish, English, Welsh, German, Dutch, and Swedish descent. From the 1830s to the 1860s, Missouri's population almost doubled with every decade.

Most of the newcomers were Americans, but many came from Germany, Ireland, Italy, and other European nations. By 1842 St. Louis was home to an Orthodox Jewish community of about 100 people. One historian believes this group can be traced back to Poland, Bohemia, and possibly England. The end of the 1800s brought even more new faces to the state. Missouri became a melting pot of people from different cultures, searching for better lives. The trend continues to this day.

> ## In Their Own Words
>
> *Being the gateway to a large city, St. Louis, I had felt from the very beginning that somehow this building should symbolize this sense of being a gateway.*
>
> —Minoru Yamsaki, Architect, St. Louis Air Terminal, Lambert-St. Louis International Airport

The people of Missouri come from a variety of different backgrounds.

The Missouri wine industry, first introduced to the state by German immigrants, is today responsible for supporting over 14,000 jobs across the state.

Population of Missouri in 2010

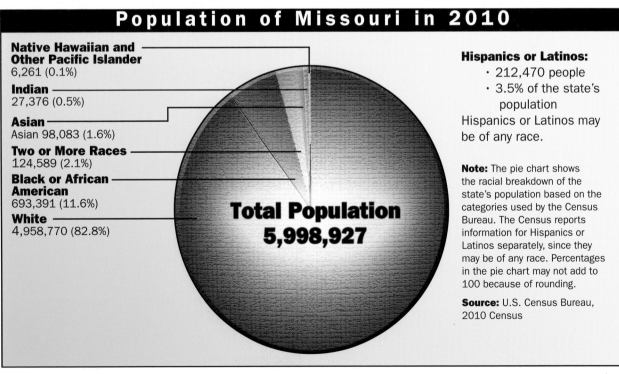

Native Hawaiian and Other Pacific Islander
6,261 (0.1%)

Indian
27,376 (0.5%)

Asian
Asian 98,083 (1.6%)

Two or More Races
124,589 (2.1%)

Black or African American
693,391 (11.6%)

White
4,958,770 (82.8%)

Total Population 5,998,927

Hispanics or Latinos:
- 212,470 people
- 3.5% of the state's population

Hispanics or Latinos may be of any race.

Note: The pie chart shows the racial breakdown of the state's population based on the categories used by the Census Bureau. The Census reports information for Hispanics or Latinos separately, since they may be of any race. Percentages in the pie chart may not add to 100 because of rounding.

Source: U.S. Census Bureau, 2010 Census

African Americans have been a key part of the state's history from its earliest days.

African Americans

People of African descent first settled in Missouri in 1764 when Pierre Lacélde founded the trading post and village that would one day be the city of St. Louis. Both slaves and free men and women made their place in the new community. According to the 1799 census, the first accurate count taken, the city's population included 56 free Africans and African Americans, 268 slaves, and 601 people of European descent.

RECIPE FOR OZARK PUDDING

Many of the settlers who first came to Missouri made their homes in the Ozarks. Follow these instructions to make a tasty treat popular in the Ozark region.

WHAT YOU NEED

2 eggs

1/2 cup flour

1 cup brown sugar

1 1/2 teaspoons baking powder

1/3 teaspoon salt

2 teaspoons vanilla extract

1/2 cup chopped nuts
(walnuts or pecans)

3/4 cup chopped apples
(peeled and cored)

In a small bowl, mix the eggs and sugar together. Be sure to beat the mixture well. Combine the flour, salt, sugar, and baking powder into a large mixing bowl. Mix these dry ingredients well and stir in the egg and sugar mixture. Add the apples, vanilla, and nuts to your batter.

Lightly grease a 10-inch-(25.4 cm) pie tin and carefully pour your batter into the tin. Put the pudding in the oven and bake for 35 minutes at 350°F (177°C). Have an adult help you with the oven. Be very careful—the pudding will be hot!

When you are done cooking the pudding, it can be served cold or warm with whipped cream, cookies, cake, or ice cream.

George Washington Carver, seen here is 1925, promoted the development of over 100 products made from peanuts.

African-American Missourians have played a major role in shaping the history of their state from its earliest days. As slaves, settlers, farmers, and soldiers, African Americans continued to leave their mark on the state throughout the 1800s. By the 1830s, they made up almost 18 percent of the state population, and their numbers were growing. After the Civil War, small African-American communities sprang up in what is known as the Little Dixie region of central Missouri. These towns grew out of a newfound freedom and a desire for land, security, and a sense of independence. One of these towns was known as Little Africa. It was located on a rugged stretch of land southwest of the town of Roanoke, in Howard County. By the late 1870s, African-American settlers owned more than 300 acres (121 ha), almost doubling that amount by the end of the century. Eventually more and more houses were built in Little Africa. A church, a school, and neighborhoods appeared. Mostly farmers, the town residents took advantage of the wealth that had come to the region from growing tobacco. By the early 1900s, though, tobacco production decreased, and

Walt Disney: Animator and Producer

Though born in Chicago, Walt Disney spent most of his childhood in Missouri, first in Marceline and then in Kansas City. He developed a love of drawing and of trains while in Marceline, where the Atchison, Topeka, and Santa Fe Railway passed through. In 1923 he founded the Walt Disney Company, which today is one of the largest media companies in the world, producing films, television shows, music, and much more.

Mark Twain: Author

Samuel Clemens, better known as Mark Twain, was born in Florida, Missouri, in 1835 and grew up in Hannibal. Before turning to writing, he spent several years as a riverboat captain traveling up and down the Mississippi River. Writing under the name Mark Twain, he was known for his ability to capture the humor and warmth of small-town life. His novels *The Adventures of Tom Sawyer* and *The Adventures of Huckleberry Finn* remain American classics.

Jesse James: Outlaw

James was born in Kearney in 1847. After fighting in the Civil War, he and his brother, Frank, pulled off their first bank robbery. For the next fifteen years, the terrible twosome wandered throughout the United States, continuing to rob banks and trains. In 1882, members of his own gang shot and killed James in order to claim the reward for his capture.

Sheryl Crow: Musician

Sheryl Crow was born in Kennett in 1962. She received her bachelor's degree from the University of Missouri and while in college, taught music at an elementary school in Fenton. She began singing in a local band and recording commercial jingles. Today, the Grammy-award winner has sold more than 50 million albums around the world!

George Washington Carver: Scientist and Inventor

George Washington Carver was born into slavery in Diamond around the time of the Civil War. At the time, most farmers in the area grew cotton, which was depleting the soil and was often destroyed by the boll weevil. Carver wanted to help farmers find other crops to grow. He researched and promoted soybeans, sweet potatoes, and most important, peanuts.

Laura Ingalls Wilder: Author

Born in Wisconsin, this author of beloved children's books lived in South Dakota, Minnesota, and Florida, before settling permanently near Mansfield, Missouri, in July 1894. Toward the end of her life, she began to write, recording the hardships and joys she experienced on the frontier. Starting with the 1932 publication of *Little House in the Big Woods*, Wilder penned a series of classic tales based on her own life that are much loved to this day.

the life of the town began to decline with it. Although by 1920 Little Africa was little more than a ghost town, it stands as a bold new experiment in freedom and a symbol of Missouri's strong, independent African-American community.

Today African Americans make up more than 11 percent of the state's population. Large communities are found in Missouri's cities—St. Louis in particular. Since arriving in Missouri, African Americans have made many important contributions to their state.

Missouri Today

Descendants of Missouri's German immigrants make up the largest ethnic group living in the state today. A German presence can be felt in pockets across the state, especially in towns such as Hermann to the west of St. Louis. Many German settlers came to this part of the state and spread out along the Missouri

These young girls perform traditional songs to honor and celebrate their German heritage.

River valley. Some immigrants sought out this area of the state because it reminded them of their homeland, in particular the stately Rhine River valley. Just like in that region of Germany, a winemaking industry quickly developed in Missouri's "Little Rhine" region. This was just one of the many traditions and pursuits the German settlers brought with them.

Among the rest of Missouri's residents of European ancestry, about one-fifth are Irish, and one-sixth claim English heritage. However, native-born Missourians trace their roots to many other nations, too.

Though Native Americans once made up the largest population in the state, today their numbers are far smaller. The most recent census showed that less than 1 percent of the population is Native American. Though that accounts for

A small but proud part of life in the Show-Me State today, Missouri's Native Americans honor the state's first residents.

Many generations of Hispanic families have made Missouri their home.

a tiny portion of the state's residents, Missouri's Native Americans are still a strong presence. Throughout the year, many observe traditional holidays and events. Across the state, several Native American groups hold festivals and other celebrations honoring their history and heritage.

Missouri also has large populations of new immigrants who add even more diversity to the Show-Me State. At Sigel Elementary School in south St. Louis, for example, students from Somalia, China, Bosnia, Mexico, and Vietnam learn alongside the school's mostly African-American students.

These newcomers have increased the presence of minorities in the state. While in 1960 there were only 3,000 Asians living in Missouri, today there are over 100,000. Latinos are another fast-growing group. Today they make up nearly 4 percent of the state's population.

In the late 1990s, many Bosnians came to Missouri to escape the fighting in their homeland in eastern Europe. When Denis Zijadic, a Bosnian immigrant, moved to Missouri in 1999, he chose to live near the Don Bosco Community

Center, in Kansas City. It was one of the places in the city that helped refugees adjust to life in America. When he bought his first home in 2001, he chose Gladstone, a community close to North Kansas City's growing Bosnian population. "You want to be close to people in your community," he said. "If you need help, it's easier to ask people from your country."

Zijadic and his family were just three of the approximately 80,000 foreign-born people who moved to Missouri in the 1990s. Most settle in Missouri's larger urban centers or in the southwestern part of the state, where jobs are easier to find. Today in the state there are about 229,000 foreign-born residents. They add their own culture and traditions to the colorful tapestry that is life in Missouri today.

Asian Americans make up about 2 percent of the state's population and own nearly 10,000 business across Missouri.

Calendar of Events

★ **Branson's Ozark Mountain Christmas**

This annual celebration begins in November and lasts through New Year's Eve. The city lights up with the Branson Area Festival of Lights. There are music performances, parades, Christmas tree lightings, and fireworks.

★ **Pony Express Pumpkinfest**

This fun-filled event, which kicks off every fall in St. Joseph, features rides, games, a parade, and a petting zoo. They all lead up to the main event, a 20-foot (6 m) wall of more than 750 carved and lighted jack-o'-lanterns called the Great Pumpkin Mountain.

★ **Greater Ozarks Blues Festival**

Each September, Springfield plays host to some of the nation's leading blues musicians. The performances are held throughout the city, on outdoor stages and in various downtown clubs.

★ **Neosho Fall Festival Autumn Harvest**

During this annual fair, festival goers are treated to arts and crafts, a Soap Box Derby, and musical performances.

★ **"Trick or Treat" Through Missouri History**

This family-friendly event, held in Columbia, is presented by the State Historical Society of Missouri. Kids and their parents are invited to come in costume to learn about crafts, bats, pumpkins, and of course, the ghosts of Missouri's past!

★ **Heritage Festival & Craft Show**

This Columbia event celebrates Missouri's proud heritage each September. While traditional crafters and tradesman demonstrate their "lost arts," there are musical performances, chuckwagons, ghost stories, and an area where kids can learn how to milk a cow, braid a rope, and make a candle!

★ Japanese Festival

This annual St. Louis event is held at the beautiful Missouri Botanical Garden. It features authentic Japanese food, music, and dancing plus tours of the Japanese garden, a martial-arts demonstration, and Taiko drumming, a central part of many Japanese celebrations.

★ Heart of America Shakespeare Festival

Held each June and July in Kansas City's Southmoreland Park, this theatrical fair is one of America's largest free Shakespeare festivals. In addition to a performance of one of the Bard's plays, audience members can also attend skits, comedy acts, and lectures.

★ Fair Saint Louis

The Gateway City hosts this three-day event known as one of the best Fourth of July celebrations in the country. Top musical acts perform on the riverfront, all as a warm-up to a spectacular fireworks display with the Gateway Arch as a backdrop.

★ Kansas City Blues Fest

This outdoor festival, presented by the Kansas City Blues Society, celebrates Missouri's unique musical traditions. Along with musical performances throughout the day, there are boat rides, food sampling, and a bonfire at the end of the night.

HARRY S. TRUMAN
1884 – 1972
PRESIDENT
OF THE
UNITED STATES

How the Government Works

Missouri's state constitution was adopted in 1945. The state had three earlier versions, each approved in 1820, 1865, and 1875. This series of constitutions shows that the state is flexible and able to change with the times. Each year brings new challenges and issues that the lawmakers and citizens of Missouri must face and solve. In order to do that, Missourians work together. They know that in order to improve life for all the state's residents, they must be open to new ideas and opinions. In Missouri politics, compromise is key.

Local Leaders

Missourians serve in their state government at all levels. Voters in each of the state's 114 counties choose local leaders, who are in charge of the day-to-day business of running Missouri's cities and towns. To be sure things run smoothly, a variety of officials are needed. Voters typically elect county commissioners, treasurers and tax collectors, coroners, sheriffs, and attorneys, just to name a few. Missouri's larger urban centers also select mayors and city councils to address the city's affairs.

Harry Truman is the only president to have hailed from the Show-Me State—so far.

The state capitol was destroyed by fire in 1837 and 1911. This version, the third, was completed in 1917. One of the building's main attractions is the murals by artist Thomas Hart Benton that decorate the House Lounge.

From Bill to Law

Ideas for laws often come directly from the people. Citizens can contact their elected officials and share their ideas on how to improve life in their state. Bills may be introduced to the legislature by either senators or representatives in the state assembly. When the bill is proposed, it is assigned a number and its title is read to the lawmakers. The bill is then sent to a committee. A committee is a small group of legislators who look into the bill more closely. They also hold a public hearing. That way, the people of Missouri have the chance to express their opinions and tell the lawmakers how they feel about the potential new law. After all, laws affect the lives of everyone in the state. Missouri's legislators want to be sure everyone has had their say.

When the public hearing is over, the committee meets to vote. If they are in favor of the bill, they send it back to either the senate or the house of representatives—whichever part of the assembly first proposed it. If they have made some changes to certain parts of the bill, then the house and the senate must consider and debate those changes as well. The bill is then placed on what is called the "perfection calendar." When its turn comes in the order of business, the bill is debated. Lawmakers consider its good points and those areas that still

Branches of Government

EXECUTIVE ★ ★ ★ ★ ★ ★ ★ ★

The governor is the head of the executive branch. He or she is elected to a four-year term and can only serve for two terms. Aiding the governor are important officials who help run the state. They include the lieutenant governor, the secretary of state, the state treasurer, and the attorney general.

LEGISLATIVE ★ ★ ★ ★ ★ ★ ★ ★

The state legislature is known as the General Assembly. It has two parts. The senate has 34 members, while the house of representatives is made up of 163. Senators serve for four years, and representatives serve for two. They help to create the laws that are needed to make Missouri run smoothly.

JUDICIAL ★ ★ ★ ★ ★ ★ ★ ★ ★

The state's highest court, the supreme court, is made up of seven justices, or judges. The state courts of appeals are divided into three districts. In addition, the state has circuit courts, associate circuit courts, and municipal courts. These lower courts handle a wide range of cases.

need to be improved. When the bill and all its amendments, or changes, have been accepted, a vote is then taken to declare the bill perfected. That means that a majority of the legislators are happy with the bill.

After the bill is perfected it is then read and voted on again. This extra step gives Missouri's lawmakers another chance to be sure the bill is a good measure for the state to adopt. If the bill passes this additional vote, it is then sent to the other half of Missouri's legislature. There it begins the same process all over again. The lawmakers form a committee, hold a hearing, and then hold a series of votes. If they request changes to the bill, both halves of the legislature must approve those changes. When the bill is in its final form and the entire legislature is happy with its terms, it is declared "truly agreed to and finally passed." The speaker of the house and the president of the senate then sign the bill.

This statue of Thomas Jefferson stands on the capitol grounds. The United States's third president also lent his name to the state capital, Jefferson City.

Next, the bill goes to the governor. If the governor signs it, the bill officially becomes a law. However, if the governor vetoes, or rejects, the bill, it then goes back to the legislature. Two-thirds of the members of each house must still be in favor of the bill to overturn the governor's veto and to make it into a law.

Getting Involved

In communities across Missouri, students have become actively involved in shaping their state. They have even proposed measures that were eventually approved by the legislature. Most of these measures have involved the adoption of official state symbols. Schoolchildren in Lee's Summit were responsible for getting the crinoid adopted as the state fossil. Marshfield's schoolchildren had the paddlefish named the state's aquatic animal, while students in Glasgow saw the channel catfish approved as the state's official fish. The Eastern black walnut became the state tree nut when, in 1990, Stockton's fourth graders drafted the bill.

In addition to signing bills into law, Missouri's governor also has many other important responsibilities. The governor appoints people to serve on many of the state's boards and commissions. He or she can also appoint someone to fill a vacancy in one of the state's US Senate seats if a senator is unable to finish a term of office. The governor also commands the state's National Guard, prepares a budget for the state, and grants pardons.

The lieutenant governor's job is to take over the job of governor if the governor is unable to finish his or her term. The lieutenant governor also leads the state senate and casts a vote in case of a tie.

Contacting Lawmakers

★ ★ ★ ★ ★ ★ ★ ★ ★ ★ ★ ★

If you are interested in contacting Missouri's state legislators, go to

http://www.moga.mo.gov

There you will find links that lead to the contact information for state senators and representatives.

Making a Living

Missouri's location has helped create a strong state economy. The state is in the middle of the nation with major waterways found in or nearby. Ever since French trappers first braved the untamed wilds of east-central Missouri, St. Louis has been an important center for transportation and trade. In the years since, banking and manufacturing also blossomed in the area. Kansas City, on the other hand, built its wealth on agriculture. Cattle and grain have been processed and sold there since the 1800s.

The state's industries are not found only within its major urban centers, though. To the southwest, cities such as Springfield are among the state's fastest growing. Many businesses have been drawn to the area through the years. Now the region sports a thriving trade in telecommunications, transportation, and warehouse-related businesses.

On the other side of the state, in southeastern Missouri, Cape Girardeau is ideally located. Its position along the Mississippi River makes it another important center for shipping and commerce. No matter where Missouri's citizens are employed, they work hard to make sure their state will continue to succeed.

Kansas City has become a major center for business and tourism.

Missouri's Industries and Workers (May 2013)

Industry	Number of People Working in That Industry	Percentage of Labor Force Working in That Industry
Farming	109,300	3.9%
Mining and Logging	4,200	0.1%
Construction	108,500	3.9%
Manufacturing	249,400	8.9%
Trade, Transportation, and Utilities	519,800	18.5%
Information	56,200	2%
Financial Activities	166,800	6%
Professional & Business Services	338,300	12%
Education & Health Services	418,100	14.9%
Leisure & Hospitality	283,900	10.1%
Other Services	113,700	4%
Government	436,900	15.6%
Totals	**2,805,100**	**99.9%**

Notes: Figures above do not include people in the armed forces.
"Professionals" includes people such as doctors and lawyers.

Source: U.S. Bureau of Labor Statistics

Farming

Missouri is farm country. About two-thirds of the state is covered with farms. About 59,000 farms raise livestock, one of Missouri's biggest products. Missouri is one of the nation's leading producers of beef cattle, pigs, and turkeys. Most cattle and hog farms are located north of the Missouri River as well as in the western and southwestern portions of the state. Dairy farms are grouped there as well. Most of the state's turkey farms are located in central Missouri.

Soybeans and corn are the state's other major crops, with much of the corn being used to feed the state's livestock. Soybean farms are found mostly on the Northern Plains, north of the Missouri River. Corn thrives across the state, but most farms are located in central Missouri, while the sorghum district is more to the east. Hay, wheat, cotton, peaches, apples, and grapes are also key Show-Me State crops.

Mining

In the early days of the territory, mining helped to make Missouri strong. Galena, a type of lead ore, was first unearthed near Potosi in 1701. Since the 1720s, with the discovery of major deposits at Mine La Motte, near Fredericktown, its importance has only grown. Mines sprang up throughout the southeastern portion of the state, which became unofficially known as the lead district. From 1870 to 1965, almost all of the state's lead came from there. At the same time, large amounts of zinc were produced from this area as well. Zinc, along with copper and silver, is collected when the iron ore is processed.

Today Missouri continues to be a mining leader. The state accounts for about 80 percent of the nation's total lead production. Since the 1960s, though, the industry has found newer and richer deposits of galena in an area now called the Viburnum Trend, located to the west of the old lead district. The state also ranks

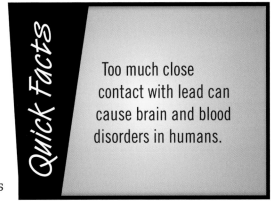

Quick Facts

Too much close contact with lead can cause brain and blood disorders in humans.

A welder sends out a shower of sparks in this Kansas City factory. The production of large-scale transportation equipment is big business in Missouri.

high in the production of fireclay, lime, cement, and crushed stone. The cement and stone usually come from Missouri's limestone quarries found along the Mississippi River. Oil, gas, and coal are produced in smaller amounts, but vital to the state's economy as well.

Iron mining is a fairly new development in Missouri. The Pea Ridge Mine, near Sullivan, was developed in the 1950s. Though companies operating the mine have faced financial difficulties, new investors recently reopened the mine and, in May 2011, opened a new magnetite processing plant as well.

Manufacturing

Over the past few decades, thousands of manufacturers have opened or expanded their businesses in the Show-Me State. These new and larger ventures have joined the several major companies already located in the state. Many of these giants are considered leaders in their field. Some Missouri companies specialize in technology related to research on genes, the information that is stored inside cells. Each of these industries requires sharp, well-trained workers, and business leaders know those workers can be found in Missouri. Other Missouri cities and towns host their own major business ventures. Kansas City is the home to the headquarters of Hallmark Cards. The next time you send or receive a birthday card, there is a good chance it was created in western Missouri.

Because Kansas City lies at the heart of the Winter Wheat Belt, there are several large flour mills in the area as well. Major automakers also have plants sprinkled across the state. Ford, General Motors, and Chrysler have helped to

Telephone operators, busy at their workstations, work at a large call center. Employers are drawn to the state's hardworking and highly qualified workforce.

CARDIFF HILL

THIS IS THE FOOT OF CARDIFF HILL, MADE FAMOUS IN MARK TWAIN'S BOOKS, "TOM SAWYER" AND "HUCKLEBERRY FINN". ON THE HILL TOM, HUCK AND THEIR GANG PLAYED AND ROAMED AT WILL.

1934

Many people visit Missouri for its historic sites. This plaque in Hannibal honors author Mark Twain.

make Missouri a leading producer of transportation equipment. Each day workers produce barges, railroad cars, truck trailers, and the bodies of automobiles. Chemicals are also big business in the state. Missouri factories pump out paint, health products, soap, and insect sprays for farms and gardens.

Retail and Services

Most of Missouri's earnings come from its service workers. They include doctors, nurses, hotel and office workers, and many others. Retail sales are also important to Missouri's economy. With such a heavily agricultural state, it is not surprising that the sale of machines and farm-related equipment is important to Missouri's economy. Other leading retail areas include restaurants, shopping malls, and car dealers. Adding to the state's earning power are bankers, real-estate agents, teachers, railroad and barge workers, and telephone company employees, to name just a few of the countless ways Missourians earn a living.

In recent years, tourism has played a larger role in building the state's wealth. Missouri is home to several professional athletic teams. Money spent on tickets to the games and souvenirs helps the state economy. The state's economy is also helped by the money people spend while staying at hotels, shopping in stores, and dining in Missouri's eateries. Branson, a resort town outside of Springfield, draws top performers, some of whom have built permanent theaters in the town. Tour buses roll through the area, filled with eager visitors. Big cities such as St. Louis offer many attractions for tourists. These include the Gateway Arch, Union Station, Forest Park, the St. Louis Zoo, and many museums. Kansas City offers visitors more miles (km) of boulevards than Paris and more fountains than any city except for Rome.

The stately Gateway Arch stands watch along the St. Louis waterfront.

Products & Resources

Cattle

Missouri ranks among the leading producers of beef cattle. The livestock industry is centered in the southwestern portion of the state. Cattle provide much of the income for the state's livestock farmers.

Soybeans

Soybeans are the state's most important crop. They are used mostly to feed livestock. They are also used in making oil. The greatest number of soybeans are produced in the northern portion of the state.

Transportation Equipment

Claycomo and Wentzville are home to two of the state's major automobile plants. Cars, trucks, bus bodies, and truck trailers are turned out every day by the state's workers.

Lead

Missouri is the nation's top producer of lead. The metal is the state's most valuable mineral. It is mostly found in the southeastern portions of the state in Iron, Reynolds, and Washington counties.

Corn

Corn has become a major crop in Missouri, with about 400 million bushels of corn produced each year. In 2011, the corn industry sustained 65,960 jobs and contributed $4.3 billion to the state's economy. Some of the state's corn is used to make ethanol, which can be used as fuel.

Pet Food

St. Louis is a leading provider of pet foods. Purina makes and distributes food for hungry dogs and all sorts of pets and farm animals. Smaller companies in other parts of the state also make sure America's animals do not go hungry.

Johnson's Shut-Ins State Park is a popular spot for residents and tourists alike.

People also come to the state to enjoy Missouri's natural wonders. Throughout the year, visitors fish, hike, and explore the different parts of the state. The Ozarks in particular have been a top destination for visitors from around the United States and around the world.

The state's residents know there is much that makes Missouri special. They look to their state with a sense of pride, and they stand committed to making it the best it can be.

State Flag & Seal

Red, white, and blue stripes cross the state flag. They stand for Missouri's pride at being a part of the Union. In the center of the flag is the state seal. Surrounding that are twenty-four stars. They show that Missouri was the twenty-fourth state.

Two grizzly bears hold a shield. They stand for the strength and bravery of the state's residents. The edge of the shield reads, "United We Stand Divided We Fall" while inside there are symbols of both the state and the nation. Missouri's state motto, "The welfare of the people shall be supreme law," appears in Latin beneath the bears.

Missouri State Map

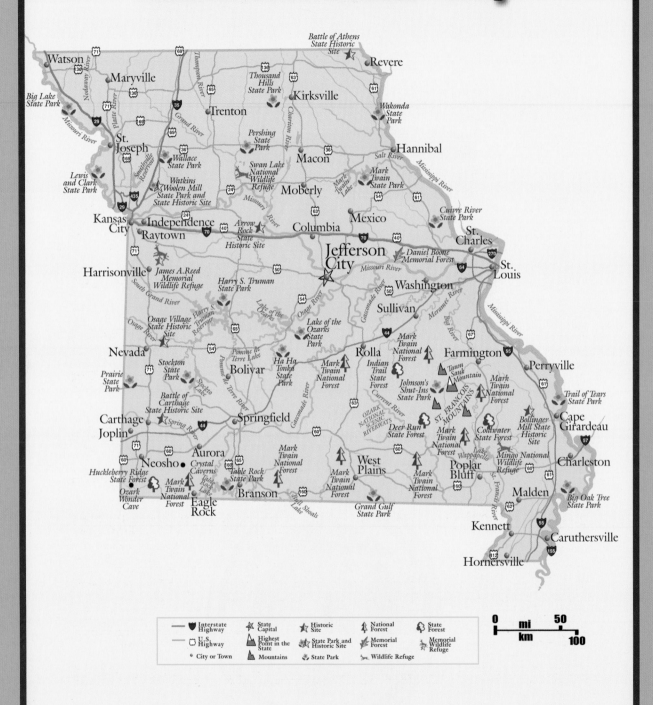

Watson
Maryville
Big Lake State Park
St. Joseph
Lewis and Clark State Park
Kansas City
Independence
Raytown
Harrisonville

Trenton
Thousand Hills State Park
Pershing State Park
Swan Lake National Wildlife Refuge
Wallace State Park
Watkins Woolen Mill State Park and State Historic Site

Kirksville
Macon
Moberly
Columbia

Battle of Athens State Historic Site
Revere
Wakonda State Park
Hannibal
Mark Twain State Park
Mark Twain Lake

Mexico
Cuivre River State Park

Jefferson City
Daniel Boone Memorial Forest
St. Charles
St. Louis

Arrow Rock State Historic Site

James A. Reed Memorial Wildlife Refuge
Harry S. Truman State Park

Washington
Sullivan

Nevada
Osage Village State Historic Site
Stockton State Park
Prairie State Park
Battle of Carthage State Historic Site

Bolivar
Ha Ha Tonka State Park
Lake of the Ozarks State Park

Rolla
Mark Twain National Forest
Indian Trail State Forest
Johnson's Shut-Ins State Park

Farmington
Taum Sauk Mountain
ST. FRANCOIS MOUNTAINS
Mark Twain National Forest

Perryville
Trail of Tears State Park
Cape Girardeau

Carthage
Joplin
Neosho
Huckleberry Ridge State Forest
Ozark Wonder Cave

Springfield
Aurora
Crystal Caverns
Mark Twain National Forest
Table Rock State Park
Branson
Eagle Rock

OZARK NATIONAL SCENIC RIVERWAYS
Deer Run State Forest

West Plains
Mark Twain National Forest

Mark Twain National Forest
Poplar Bluff
Coldwater State Forest
Bollinger Mill State Historic Site
Mingo National Wildlife Refuge
Lake Wappapello

Charleston
Malden
Big Oak Tree State Park

Kennett
Caruthersville

Grand Gulf State Park
Hornersville

Legend
- Interstate Highway
- U.S. Highway
- City or Town
- State Capital
- Highest Point in the State
- Mountains
- Historic Site
- State Park and Historic Site
- State Park
- National Forest
- Memorial Forest
- Wildlife Refuge
- State Forest
- Memorial Wildlife Refuge

mi 0 50
km 100

The Missouri Waltz

words by James Royce, music by Frederic Knight Logan

BOOKS

Cromwell, Sharon. *Dred Scott v. Sanford: A Slave's Case for Freedom and Citizenship.* Snapshots in History. North Mankato, MN: Compass Point Books, 2009.

Lago, Mary Ellen. *Missouri.* From Sea to Shining Sea. Danbury, CT: Children's Press, 2009.

Lanier, Wendy. *What Was the Missouri Compromise?: And Six Other Questions About the Struggle over Slavery.* Six Questions of American History. Minneapolis, MN: Lerner Publishing Group, 2012.

Marsico, Katie. *The Missouri River.* Explorer Library: Social Studies Explorer. North Mankato, MN: Cherry Lake Publishing, 2013.

WEBSITES

Office of Missouri Governor
http://governor.mo.gov

Official Missouri State Website
http://www.mo.gov

Xplor/Missouri Department of Conservation
http://xplor.mdc.mo.gov

Doug Sanders is a writer living in New York City. He attended graduate school in St. Louis, where he loved going to Blues games and eating Ted Drewe's frozen custard. While not in the city, he enjoyed visiting other parts of Missouri, including Montauk State Park and Johnson's Shut-Ins.